# NaGL (Not a Good Look)

Lech Mackiewicz

Currency Press,
Sydney

METANOIA

CURRENT THEATRE SERIES

First published in 2015
by Currency Press Pty Ltd,
PO Box 2287, Strawberry Hills, NSW, 2012, Australia
enquiries@currency.com.au
www.currency.com.au

in association with Metanoia Theatre Company



Cataloguing-in-publication data for this title is available from the National Library of Australia website: www.nla.gov.au

Typeset by Dean Nottle for Currency Press.
Printed by Fineline Print + Copy Service, St Peters.
Cover shows Greg Ulfan.
Cover designed by Matthias Lanz, Loupe Studio.
Cover photographs by Deryk McAlpin from Proof.

# Contents

*NaGL* was first produced by Auto Da Fe Theatre Company at the Tap Gallery, Sydney, on 30 August 2010, with the following cast:

| | |
|---|---|
| UNCLE CHUK | Billy McPherson |
| MANOLO | Keith Alexander |
| GRACE | Jennie Dibley |
| VATA | Malina Mackiewicz<br>Sophia Scarpellino<br>(for three performances) |
| ROMAN | Tom Pelik |

Director and Designer, Lech Mackiewicz
Associate Director, Tom Pelik
Assistant Director, Izabella Mackiewicz
Lighting, Larry Kelly
Sound, Inna Klyuchnikova
Producer, Tracey Adams
Artwork Design, Jurek Szafjanski
Stage Manager, Tess Moffat-Sosa

## CHARACTERS

MANOLO, 45 or 75 or even 85 years old; rather big, bearish in appearance but very delicate in his mannerisms, so his rude remarks sound odd and out of place (he can be tiny in his appearance if the role of his wife—Grace—is cast by a large woman); untidy, longish hair; uses an Italian accent at times but very rarely.

GRACE, 44 or 74 or even 84 years old; rather tiny and skinny but very strong in her attitude and manners; her leadership qualities should be in direct contrast to her physical appearance (she may be big if Manolo is small—ideally Manolo and Grace should be physically at two extreme ends of the appearance scale); very tidy, obsessively clean and thus cleaning obsessively; full Ozzie accent.

ROMAN BOLDING, circa 30 years old, with moustache and heavy Eastern European accent; uncertain of anything; switches to Ozzie accent at times—it's more the way he pronounces certain words (like: 'hello') in a very Australian way rather than the whole sentence; he wants to impress Vata, his sister.

VATA, attractive blond with exaggerated American accent; looks fit; not skinny!; younger than her brother Roman, but dominant; well-organised; she doesn't like to stop, so she keeps exercising at any given opportunity (Vata can be a screaming redhead as an alternative—in any case, her hair is a statement).

UNCLE CHUK, Aboriginal; ageless, with beard and dignity; but the dignity is diluted by his lack of confidence paired with his self-inflicted destructive determination to please the others, but… don't be misled by his appearance, because when he forgets his limitations he can be deadly: fast, strong and invincible… Uncle Chuk!

## SETTING

Partly a boxing ring and partly a very busy (*very busy!*) living area of a heavily furnished family apartment. Some furniture is stacked up the walls, some furniture climbs the walls and some hangs upside down from the walls and ceiling creating a very disturbed perspective. Unsettling for the viewers.

The ring and the apartment 'crossfade'.

The ring is being occupied by Uncle Chuk, who sits in the corner as if a boxing trainer who observes the actions of the other members of this unholy family. Uncle Chuk introduces all eighteen rounds of this ill-matched Full-On Theatre Bout by reading out the title of each round from the call cards and starting each round by ringing the ring bell. He is our Master of Ceremonies. And before he starts the Bout, he pays respect to the traditional owners of the land, where this Full-On Theatre Bout is to be staged!

# FIRST STANZA

*The stage is in darkness.*

*Gong!*

*Lights up.*

*ROUND ONE*

UNCLE CHUK *holds up a call card on which is written: 'Round 1: Little pimple on Earth's dirty bum'.*

UNCLE CHUK: Round number one: Little pimple on Earth's dirty bum. Round number one: Little pimple on Earth's dirty bum. Round number one: Little pimple on Earth's dirty bum.

*Lights down.*

*A door (stage right) slowly opens. A stream of light cuts across the stage revealing a space full of furniture that could be anything, but most likely is a dining/living room.*

*The sound of heavy steps approaching the open door grows in volume. A large backlit male figure appears in the doorway and stops, casting a shadow across the space. It is* MANOLO.

*Pause.*

MANOLO: Up your arse!

*He giggles and tiptoes away, scared. There is no reaction to his action. Nothing happens. He creeps back, assuming his position in the doorway.*

*Pause.*

Up your…

*A door on the opposite side swings open with a bang.* MANOLO *giggles, turns and runs for his life, slamming the door closed behind himself.*

*A small female figure steps into the doorway (stage left). She casts a small shadow across the space. She is* GRACE. *She holds a spatula in her raised hand.*

GRACE: Shut up! You scared little piece of shit!

MANOLO*'s giggle can be heard offstage.*

Shut the fuck up!

MANOLO *explodes with more laughter.*

I swear to God, I'll give it to you!

*Silence.*

GRACE *waits, uncertain. She raises the spatula and shakes it with anger.*

You're asking for it! You little swollen pimple on Earth's dirty bum!

*The door (stage right) opens slowly again.* MANOLO *assumes his position. They stand like that for a while.*

MANOLO: That was a good one.

GRACE *raises the spatula higher.*

GRACE: Shush! You little fart.

MANOLO *chuckles.*

MANOLO: '... pimple on Earth's bum!'
GRACE: Pimple, what?
MANOLO: Pimple was good.

GRACE *jumps and stomps her feet three times.* MANOLO *squats. Nothing happens.*

*Pause.*

GRACE: Shush! You little pimple!

MANOLO *bends over towards* GRACE *and whispers as if prompting:*

MANOLO: '... on the Earth's dirty bum'!
GRACE: I know!
MANOLO: So say it.
GRACE: Say what?
MANOLO: What I have said... just then.
GRACE: And what did you say?

MANOLO: I said what you had said before… about—

GRACE *cuts in.*

GRACE: So, I said it, right?
MANOLO: What?
GRACE: I say, I said it.
MANOLO: Said, what?
GRACE: What you want me to say now?!
MANOLO: [*thinking*] Yes. You said it. [*He thinks.*] But—
GRACE: [*cutting in*] Aaaaaaaaaa!

*She pauses and listens. Silence, then* MANOLO *opens his mouth.*

MANOLO: But…
GRACE: Aaaaaaaaaaaaaaaaaaa!

*She pauses and listens. Silence.* MANOLO *opens his mouth as if to talk.*

Aaaaaaaaaaaaaaaaaaaaaaaa!

*She listens. Silence.*

Aaa?
MANOLO: Okay. I got the point.
GRACE: What point?
MANOLO: Your point.
GRACE: Can you be more specific?

MANOLO *gives up and sits down.*

MANOLO: I give up. I mean it: I give up!
GRACE: [*slowly*] Fuck me dead, if I will repeat after you. Anything, you cheap piss!

MANOLO *starts laughing.*

MANOLO: That's great. Fuck you dead! That's great!

*A metal object falls to the ground offstage, making a lot of noise. They freeze.*

Quiet! It wasn't them?
GRACE: No. It was a frying pan.
MANOLO: Then, they're not here.
GRACE: No.

MANOLO: Thank God. I wasn't sure. [*Pause.*] Let's eat. Time for breakfast… Thank God… for the food.

*Blackout.*

*End of Round One.*

UNCLE CHUK *rings the bell.*

*ROUND TWO*

UNCLE CHUK *holds up a call card: 'Round 2: Give it back! It's mine!'*

UNCLE CHUK: Round two: Give it back! It's mine! Round two: Give it back! It's mine! Round two: Give it back! It's mine!

*He shadowboxes.*

*Blackout.*

UNCLE CHUK *rings the bell.*

*Lights up.*

MANOLO *and* GRACE *sit opposite each other eating quickly, looking at each other's plate. Each of them wants to finish first so the other won't have a chance to share in their dish.* MANOLO *finishes first. He rolls back and laughs.*

MANOLO: I finished first, you slow motion of a woman, you!

GRACE *slows down her eating now. She bends over and reaches for a roll that* MANOLO *left next to his plate.*

GRACE: You forgot the bread roll, speedy pants!

*She bites into it.* MANOLO *jumps up.*

MANOLO: Ouu! Give it back. It's mine!

GRACE *stuffs the bread roll in her mouth.*

GRACE: You said you finished… End. No more. *Finito!* Learn to be a man of his word, you! First!

MANOLO: I don't want to be a man of his word. Who is he anyway? I want my bread roll back.

*He starts weeping uncontrollably as* GRACE *finishes his bread roll.*

*Lights fade slowly to blackout.*

*In complete darkness:*

GRACE: Are you okay?

MANOLO*'s weeping stops abruptly.*

MANOLO: I'm better now.

UNCLE CHUK *rings the bell.*

*End of Round Two.*

*Silence.*

*Lights on* UNCLE CHUK.

*ROUND THREE*

UNCLE CHUK *holds up a call card: 'Round 3: Give me but one good reason!'*

UNCLE CHUK: Give me but one good reason! Give me but one good reason! Give me but one good reason!

*He shadowboxes.*

*He rings the bell.*

*Both doors swing open.*

ROMAN *(stage right) and* VATA *(stage left) step into the doorways.* MANOLO *and* GRACE *scream and dive under the table.* ROMAN *and* VATA *simultaneously reach for the lighting switch and turn the light on. They burst in and start imitating a boxing match, while moving towards the middle.* ROMAN *looks behind the couch.*

ROMAN: No! Not here.

VATA *looks behind the curtain.*

VATA: I don't think so.

ROMAN *looks under the carpet.*

ROMAN: How many, they said?

VATA: One.

ROMAN: Just one?

VATA: 'But one.'

ROMAN: Really? 'But one"?

VATA: [*thinking*] I think they mean more.
ROMAN: Two?
VATA: At least. It's better to be on the safe side.

ROMAN *shakes his head.*

ROMAN: What do they say, again?

VATA *stops in her boxing movements.*

VATA: 'Give me but one good reason.'
ROMAN: … 'But one'!
VATA: 'And I'll divorce thee!'

ROMAN *shakes his head again.*

ROMAN: I don't like the 'thee' word. I think it's a mistake. It should read 'they'.

*He discovers* MANOLO *and* GRACE *under the table.*

Here they are. [*He eyeballs* MANOLO.] What are you doing here? Are you hiding something from us?

MANOLO *hides behind* GRACE. ROMAN *follows him under the table.*

I asked you a question!

GRACE *crawls out and sits on the tabletop.* VATA *doesn't even look at* GRACE *and keeps searching while addressing* GRACE.

VATA: He asked you a question.
GRACE: I live here. And now let me ask you a question: What are you doing here?

ROMAN *crawls out from under the table.*

ROMAN: We're trying…

GRACE *confronts him.*

GRACE: Trying what?
VATA: [*stepping in*] We're trying to find a good reason—

MANOLO *sticks his head out and cuts in.*

MANOLO: I'll give you a good reason!

*They all turn to* MANOLO. *He freezes.*

ROMAN, VATA & GRACE: [*together*] Yes?

*Pause.*

MANOLO: Foul language.

GRACE *turns to* VATA.

GRACE: Yeah. Foul language for starters.

ROMAN *and* VATA *look at each other.* MANOLO *climbs out from under the table. They look at* MANOLO *again.*

MANOLO: Alcohol.

*They look at each other.*

GRACE: Soccer.

UNCLE CHUK: Lack of resources.

*All look at* UNCLE CHUK. *He turns away and looks at the audience.*

MANOLO: Lack of resources.

VATA: I don't get this one.

MANOLO: Okay. I don't either.

GRACE: It's money.

MANOLO, VATA & ROMAN: [*together*] Money?

GRACE: Skip it. [*Turning to* VATA] You should be taking notes, shouldn't you?

VATA: I will decide who does what here, right? You smart ass! [*To* ROMAN] You take notes.

ROMAN: Sure thing. [*To* MANOLO] What else?

MANOLO: Petrol prices.

ROMAN *starts taking notes.*

Postnatal depression.

VATA: What's this one?

*They look at each other confused.* GRACE *raises her arm.*

Yes, Grace?

GRACE: Opposite to prenatal… ecstasy… I'm sure, yes.

VATA *looks at* ROMAN.

VATA: Thank you, Grace. You can sit down. [*Pause.*] We'll go with the foul language. It reminds me of football somchow.

MANOLO: And fishing.

*He smiles.* ROMAN *looks at him and smiles, too.*

ROMAN: Yeah. Fishing…

VATA *slaps* ROMAN *on his back at the same time as* GRACE *slaps* MANOLO.

VATA: I'll show you fishing! Off we go! One good reason will do, thank you!

VATA *grabs* ROMAN*'s ear and turns him to face* GRACE *and* MANOLO.

ROMAN: If I was you I'd make sure that I'm right, because otherwise—you know.

ROMAN *shakes his fist.* VATA *pulls his ear and drags him to the table. She bangs his head rhythmically on the table while speaking, to emphasise her point.*

VATA: You see what you make him do. Keep it in mind! Because he'll be back.

*She forces* ROMAN *to go.*

ROMAN: Ouch!

*They exit through the open door (stage left).* MANOLO *and* GRACE *wait for a moment before tiptoeing to both doors and closing them simultaneously and slowly—without making any noise. They freeze-stop.*

UNCLE CHUK *rings the bell.*

*Blackout.*

*End of Round Three.*

*Lights on* UNCLE CHUK *in the ring.*

## *ROUND FOUR*

UNCLE CHUK *holds up a call card: 'Round 4: Setting the priorities right. We are all bloody Australians here!'*

UNCLE CHUK: Setting the priorities right. We are all bloody Australians here! Setting the priorities right. We are all bloody Australians here!

*He shadowboxes.*

*He rings the bell.*

GRACE *and* MANOLO *come back to life.*

GRACE: You know what worries me?

MANOLO *doesn't answer.*

That they may be…

MANOLO: I don't want to know!

GRACE: … they may be right, actually.

MANOLO: I don't want to know.

GRACE: But why?

MANOLO *doesn't answer.*

Anyway, you know 'why' already. I just told you.

MANOLO: Well: 'Let's sit down and discuss it?'

GRACE: That's exactly what I wanted to suggest. Let's assess and evaluate.

*They go and sit together on the couch.* MANOLO *bites his fist in fury.*

MANOLO: I knew it! I hate meetings, especially when you say that they may be right, 'cause you're always right, you bitch!

GRACE *smiles and strokes his hair.*

GRACE: Because you're so fuckin' continental.

MANOLO *looks at her and they both laugh and roll off the couch to the floor.*

MANOLO: Because you're so fuckin' pommyesh.

*They laugh even louder on the floor.* GRACE *stops.*

GRACE: That's the way we are. But they have it easier.

MANOLO *stops laughing and thinks.*

MANOLO: Why is that? Usually Poles have it easier.

GRACE: And aren't they so fuckin' Polish?!

*They both roll back again.*

MANOLO: And to think that we are all so fuckin' Australian! But why Poles would have it easier?

GRACE: Because they are the fuckin' chosen nation.

MANOLO: Bloody hell! Is that right? I'd think we were the chosen nation.
GRACE: Yes, why wouldn't you? Bloody hell. But they got the Pope, the Polish jokes and all. Every year a winter of a century and a new planet discovered. After the book. To the letter.

MANOLO *starts crying.*

MANOLO: What book?
GRACE: Nostradamus.

GRACE *starts sobbing.*

MANOLO: Yeah, right. You say so.

*They both cry.* MANOLO *looks to* GRACE.

Why are you crying, you idiot?
GRACE: That's because of the bloody Australians.
MANOLO: Bloody Australians—what?
GRACE: They don't realise how lucky they are!

*She wails.*

MANOLO: But we are the bloody Australians! [*He jumps up and down—furious.*] Holy shit! Holy shit! You don't say! What do we do about it?
GRACE: I don't know.
MANOLO: Neither do I.
GRACE: You see. We don't know.
MANOLO: Wait. I know.
GRACE: But you don't realise!
MANOLO: I don't realise, but I know. Get up.

*He pulls* GRACE *right up. He stands with his hand on his heart. She copies him. He starts humming the national anthem. She joins in, humming gently. After one verse they finish with flair. They stand there for a while after finishing.*

That's better, mate!
GRACE: You're right. That's better, mate!
MANOLO: That's all because of the bloody wogs.
GRACE: Bloody who?
MANOLO: Bloody wogs!

GRACE *raises her hand.*

GRACE: Wow! Wow! Wow!

MANOLO *looks at her, surprised.*

MANOLO: Wow?
GRACE: You don't say bloody wogs! It's not right.
MANOLO: So, what do you say?
GRACE: You say bloody migrants.
MANOLO: [*thinking*] I don't mean bloody migrants.
GRACE: What do you mean?
MANOLO: Bloody wogs.
GRACE: No…
MANOLO: I know who I mean!
GRACE: You are getting confused…
MANOLO: You are getting confused, woman. I know who I mean. I mean: wogs.

GRACE *cries.*

GRACE: And then, they… You see, I don't like it when they call us fuckin' convicts! And they will if we cannot control ourselves and keep cool, you know.

MANOLO *comforts her.*

MANOLO: Look, you idiot: I know what I'm talking about—bloody wogs deal drugs, rape girls, abuse our values and piss on us in general.

GRACE *keeps sobbing.*

GRACE: And we give it to them, right? And they aren't the bloody migrants?
MANOLO: No. The bloody migrants are peaceful people. Just like bloody us, who go to school, who go to work, pray to their God and all they bloody want, like us, is: better life for our bloody kids. And like us they don't realise how lucky they are.

GRACE *stops crying.*

We must be strong. It's not easy for us… under the circumstances… We must eat. Have we eaten? [*He starts frantically running around.*] Oh, my God! Have we eaten, yet? Oh, fuck me dead! Have we eaten, yet?

GRACE *starts crying again.*

What? Why? What happened?

GRACE: You said: 'Fuck me dead'.

MANOLO: Yes?

GRACE: I don't want to fuck you dead.

MANOLO: [*remembering*] Didn't you say it before?

GRACE: I did. [*Pause.*] I dunno. It feels different, when I say to you: 'Fuck me dead'.

MANOLO *imagines.*

MANOLO: Fair enough. Let's eat something. I'll feel better then.

UNCLE CHUK *rings the bell.*

*Blackout.*

*End of Round Four.*

*Lights on* UNCLE CHUK *in the ring.*

*ROUND FIVE*

UNCLE CHUK *holds up a call card: 'Round 5: Jealousy'.*

UNCLE CHUK: Jealousy. Jealousy. Jealousy.

*He rings the bell.*

*As the lights come up,* MANOLO *sits at the little coffee table and stirs a hot tomato soup on his plate.* GRACE *stands motionless opposite him, watching his actions intensely.* MANOLO *glances briefly at her, fills his spoon, brings it to his mouth, but suddenly changes his mind and splashes the soup at her. She doesn't move.*

GRACE: What?

MANOLO *doesn't say a word. He stirs the soup, fills the spoon and brings it to his mouth.* GRACE *raises her hand to protect her face from a possible splash.* MANOLO *swallows the soup. She relaxes. He stirs the soup again and fills the spoon. He brings it to his mouth but changes his mind and suddenly splashes the soup at her. She is furious.*

What?!

*Pause.*

MANOLO: Nothing.

*He gets back to eating. After two spoonfuls of soup he looks at* GRACE *again and starts stirring. He slowly raises the spoon but stops short of splashing the soup at her. She jumps three times, stomping her feet loudly.*

GRACE: What? What? What?!

MANOLO: When I remember that you weren't a virgin when I took you for my wife!—I dunno—it just drives me bloody nuts!

*He gets back to eating. This time he eats furiously.* GRACE *looks at him for a while.*

GRACE: You're bloody pathetic!

MANOLO *stops eating and stands up.*

MANOLO: Am I?

GRACE: You're like that stupid man from that stupid joke.

MANOLO: Really?

*He starts pacing around the stage.*

GRACE: Yeah, really! You bloody moron!

MANOLO *stops and thinks.*

MANOLO: I can't help it. I still love you, woman!

GRACE: You better do, because who will cook for you, hey?

*She goes to take the plate.* MANOLO *tries to snatch it from her.*

MANOLO: I can cook for myself.

GRACE *turns and puts it back on the table.*

GRACE: So you can.

MANOLO *sits back.*

MANOLO: And don't you ever call me… [*thinking*] … a moron, right?

GRACE: Why?

MANOLO: And a… pathetic, right?

GRACE: And why? I ask.

MANOLO *thinks and looks up at her with steely eyes.*

MANOLO: You know what it means?

GRACE: Which one?

MANOLO: Either. You don't know what you're saying! Not at all. And it hurts.

GRACE: So, you tell me.

MANOLO *holds her gaze.*

MANOLO: No. I won't.

GRACE *bends down and steps in closer.*

GRACE: You will!
MANOLO: No. I won't!

GRACE *thinks. She comes closer and suddenly she kisses him on the lips. Then she runs around and hugs him.*

GRACE: Please.

MANOLO *hesitates.*

MANOLO: Okay. [*Pause.*] Bring me the dictionary.
GRACE: But…
MANOLO: No 'buts'. The dictionary.

GRACE *goes to the big table and dives under it. She returns with a book.* MANOLO *takes it and looks at it.*

It's not the dictionary. It's not even a dictionary. It's your bloody guide book.

*He throws the book at her. She catches it.*

GRACE: This is the only book we have.

MANOLO *shakes his head.* GRACE *waits.*

MANOLO: Well, then. It'll have to do. Let's see. [*He leafs through very quickly and finds a page.*] Look. It's right here. Found it. [*He tries to read, but gives up.*] No. You read it, so you remember better.

GRACE *takes the book from him. She reads the definitions in Italian.*

GRACE: [*in Italian*] Moron: *babbeo, stupidotto, cretino, cazzaro*. Pathetic: *miserabile, misero, patetico, penoso, pietoso, povero, sfortunato*. [*She looks up at* MANOLO.] And?

MANOLO *thinks.*

MANOLO: It's not as bad as I thought.

GRACE *jumps up.*

GRACE: Can you translate it for me, you bloody… Roman.

MANOLO *shakes his head.*

MANOLO: I'm not Roman. I'm [*thinking*] Italian.

GRACE: Are you?

MANOLO: Yeah.

GRACE: And you cannot translate?!

MANOLO: Because I live here. Not there. I'm a half-half, you know.

GRACE: So how come you can't speak a half-half language?

MANOLO: Because I can half-understand and I cannot half-speak. Two halves, you see. That makes it for a perfect me! *Perfetto mio!*

GRACE: You're a bloody… pathetic… and a fuckin' moron as well. A perfect one.

MANOLO *raises his fist.*

MANOLO: Hey, hey, woman! Hold on!

GRACE *confronts him.*

GRACE: You just said it wasn't so bad after all.

MANOLO *backs off and giggles.*

MANOLO: No, it wasn't. It was quite good actually. Bloody good! Not everyone can be a bloody pathetic, you see.

GRACE: And a bloody moron?

MANOLO: I'm not sure about that one.

GRACE: Do you think I can be a bloody pathetic, too?

MANOLO *looks at her suspiciously.*

MANOLO: If you ask nicely.

GRACE *does a curtsey and bows.*

GRACE: Please.

MANOLO *considers.*

MANOLO: All bloody right. But…

*He raises his fist.* GRACE *ducks.*

… you know.

GRACE: I know, I know, you moron.

MANOLO: Okay. So now we are both bloody pathetics.

*They sit in silence, staring ahead.*

MANOLO *gets back to eating soup. He wants to splash his soup at* GRACE *again, but he pulls back.*

I hate this bloody soup.

GRACE: It's a tomato soup.

MANOLO: I hate it.

*He keeps eating.*

UNCLE CHUK *rings the bell.*

*Blackout.*

*End of Round Five.*

*ROUND SIX*

UNCLE CHUK *holds up a call card: 'Round 6: News and TV'.*

UNCLE CHUK: News and TV. News and TV. News and TV

*He shadowboxes.*

*He rings the bell.*

*The stage is covered in darkness.*

MANOLO *(facing the audience) switches on a TV set located stage right near the centre. His face is lit by the static light coming from the screen. He mumbles a few swear words and tries to change the channel—to no avail—only static again. And the muffled noise.*

MANOLO: I hate commercial breaks.

*He switches the channel again. And again the light of an empty screen lights up his face.*

That's better, mate.

*He stares at the screen. The door stage left starts to open slowly with a squeak. A ray of light widens until it reaches* MANOLO, *who instantly turns off the television. The door closes with a slam.*

*Pause.*

*The same door flies wide open.* GRACE *steps in and freezes in the doorframe. She is holding two jugs in her outstretched arms.*

*Pause.*

GRACE: Coffee?
MANOLO: Coffee?
GRACE: Tea?
MANOLO: Tea?

GRACE *puts the light on.* MANOLO *is nowhere to be seen.*

GRACE: Coffee or tea?
MANOLO: What do you think?
GRACE: I'm asking you.
MANOLO: I don't want to be a problem…

GRACE *jumps three times, stomping her feet furiously.*

GRACE: You're not a problem, for God's sake!

MANOLO *crawls out from underneath the couch located stage left, behind* GRACE. *She turns surprised.*

Here you are. Well, then?
MANOLO: [*thinking*] … So I'll have some coffee and some tea in order to avoid any further confusion.

*He produces a cup.* GRACE *looks at it and then pours from both jugs at the same time.*

Thank you… [*thinking*] … Grace.

*He puts the cup down on the floor.* GRACE *stomps. He picks up the cup and drinks. She turns to go, but stops.*

GRACE: You've been watching television again?
MANOLO: Me? Why?
GRACE: I can tell. You're confused.
MANOLO: No I'm not. Can I have some more?

*He reaches his cup out.*

GRACE: No way. Too much drink and you'll wet yourself. [*She looks at him closely. Pause.*] Have you watched the news?

MANOLO *freezes.*

MANOLO: The news? [*He thinks.*] Yes. [*He turns to face her.*] Bloody news!
GRACE: Shocking! Isn't it?
MANOLO: Yes. Shocking. Isn't it?

GRACE: I just said it.
MANOLO: Did you?
GRACE: Yes. I did.
MANOLO: Did you? Really?
GRACE: Yes. Bloody news. Shocking!
MANOLO: There you go.

*He turns to go.*

GRACE: When did you watch it?

MANOLO *remembers.*

MANOLO: I… hang on… Last … No, the one before… No… Yeah… A few… Yes. A few years ago.

GRACE *looks him in the eyes.*

GRACE: A few years ago? [*She thinks*.] That's bloody old news!
MANOLO: Yes. Always the same.
GRACE: Nothing new?
MANOLO: No. Nothing.
GRACE: For years! Nothing new for years. [*Pause*.] What bloody 'news'? They should rename it 'olds'!

MANOLO *shakes his head.*

MANOLO: I think 'news' is good. Kind of cute. It's like someone saying: 'Don't worry—nothing's changed'.
GRACE: Or: 'There is nothing to worry about'?
MANOLO: Exactly. That's what news is about. About all the sameness: politics, murders…
GRACE: … cyclones and earthquakes…
MANOLO: … pedophiles and famine…
GRACE: … wars and endangered species…
MANOLO: … and changing weather patterns…
GRACE: Yes. You're right—
MANOLO: 'News' is good. I like 'news'.
GRACE: News is good for me. I feel safer.

MANOLO *freezes in shock.*

MANOLO: But what about football?
GRACE: You mean soccer, union, or the rules?

MANOLO: Any football.

GRACE: What about it?

MANOLO: It must be on the news! It's like… I dunno… It's a bloody must! It's a bloody pathetic!

*He still doesn't move as he tries to remember.*

GRACE: You can have your football on your bloody news, but, please, keep our pathetics to us, okay? I want to feel unique, and not just football-sized for the sake of news.

MANOLO *snaps out of his stupor.*

MANOLO: I remember: the Blues won.

GRACE: Can't be. The Blues?

MANOLO: It was on the news I watched.

GRACE: That was some years ago, but.

MANOLO: So they must be champs for all those years if nothing changes on the news, right?!

GRACE: Isn't it great to barrack for the right team?

MANOLO: And to listen to the right news.

GRACE: And to watch the right news. [*She looks around.*] Shall I put the TV on?

MANOLO: No need, really. Remember? We know the news. It's all the same, silly.

*They sit down facing the audience. After a while they smile.*

UNCLE CHUK *rings the bell.*

*Blackout.*

*End of Round Six.*

*ROUND SEVEN*

UNCLE CHUK *holds up a call card: 'Round 7: The way people see you may limit your options'.*

UNCLE CHUK: The way people see you may limit your options. The way people see you may limit your options.

*He shadowboxes.*

*He rings the bell.*

*When the lights come up* GRACE *and* MANOLO *are in the same positions: seated, smiling, and looking ahead.*

*Both doors swing open.* ROMAN *(stage right) and* VATA *(stage left) put their heads in and freeze.*

ROMAN *bursts in.*

ROMAN: Sit down! All of you!

*Nobody moves. Everyone is confused.* GRACE *breaths deeply.*

GRACE: We are seated, already.

ROMAN *turns to* GRACE.

ROMAN: Don't try to confuse me.

VATA *jumps in front of* ROMAN.

VATA: So stand up! You didn't stand up, when we got in.
GRACE: We didn't?

VATA *bends over* GRACE.

VATA: That's what I call 'a bad girl'. It's not gonna help you.
MANOLO: So what do you want us to do?
ROMAN: 'Sit down!' I said.
MANOLO: Okay, darling. Let's get up.

ROMAN *is furious and confused.*

ROMAN: No! 'Sit down!' I said.

MANOLO *is scared and confused.*

MANOLO: What about sitting up? Would that help?

ROMAN *looks at* VATA.

VATA: Up?

*She looks at* MANOLO.

MANOLO: Down?
ROMAN: Down?
VATA: Down?
ROMAN: Up?
VATA: Up?
GRACE: Look, why won't you sort it out among yourselves, alright, and I'll get us some tea? How d'you have it?

ROMAN: White. One sugar.
VATA: Black. No sugar, thanks.

GRACE *gets up.*

GRACE: Some things don't change, do they?

MANOLO *raises his arm.*

MANOLO: And a decaf latte for me.
GRACE: Couldn't be any simpler.

GRACE *exits.*

ROMAN *and* VATA *stare at* MANOLO. MANOLO *feels the pressure. He doesn't take his eyes off them and slowly starts descending backwards as if to lie down. When he is about to reach the floor,* ROMAN *jumps up.*

ROMAN: Sit up! All of you.

MANOLO *sits up.*

MANOLO: So this one's solved.

*They face-off each other in silence.*

GRACE: [*offstage*] And one more thing: You should consider the way you look, the way you dress… you know… it affects the way people see you… it may limit your options…
MANOLO, VATA & ROMAN: [*together*] What?
GRACE: [*offstage*] Not a Good Look. In short: NaGL.

MANOLO, GRACE *and* ROMAN *look at each other.*

MANOLO, VATA & ROMAN: [*together*] Who are you talking to?
GRACE: [*offstage*] Isn't that obvious? [*She giggles.*] Who wants sugar?
VATA: I don't. [*Pause.*] We've got some news for you.
MANOLO: Oh, that's good.
VATA: I'm not so sure.
MANOLO: We've just discussed the news. There's nothing to be afraid of.

*Pause.*

ROMAN: You want the bad news first or the good news first?
MANOLO: News is always good, right?
ROMAN: Shut up! Good or bad?
MANOLO: Good I guess.

ROMAN: Too bad.
MANOLO: And then you can have a go with the good one again and spare us the bad one.
ROMAN: But how?
MANOLO: Just skip it.

ROMAN *looks to* VATA.

VATA: It is kind of good news, too. He may be right after all.

ROMAN *thinks.*

Just say it.
ROMAN: The good news is: We filed for a divorce.

GRACE *comes back with a tray full of steaming cups.*

GRACE: And the good news?

ROMAN *and* VATA *look at each other.*

VATA: Okay. Tell them.
ROMAN: Okay. And the good news is: We filed for a divorce.

GRACE *and* MANOLO *look at each other.*

GRACE: But that was the first good news.
ROMAN: Yes. That's right.
VATA: They are kind of… the same.

MANOLO *looks at* GRACE. GRACE *looks at* MANOLO. *They nod in agreement.*

GRACE: You're right.
MANOLO: News are always the same.
GRACE: Nothing ever changes on the news front.

VATA *and* ROMAN *look at each other in amazement.*

VATA: You don't get it: We filed for a divorce.

GRACE *hands out the cups.*

GRACE: That's not too bad. Could be worse.

*She hands a cup to* MANOLO.

Latte for you.
MANOLO: Thank you.
GRACE: Maybe it's even good. Who knows?

ROMAN *and* VATA *take their cups.*

ROMAN & VATA: [*together*] Thanks.

*They all sit facing the audience and take a sip together.*

GRACE: So, tell me: Who are the lucky couple?

UNCLE CHUK *rings the bell.*

*Blackout.*

*End of Round Seven.*

*ROUND EIGHT*

UNCLE CHUK *holds up a call card: 'Round 8: NaGL'.*

UNCLE CHUK: NaGL. NaGL. NaGL.

*He shadowboxes.*

*He rings the bell.*

GRACE, MANOLO, ROMAN *and* VATA *sit, still staring out.*

VATA: NaGL?

GRACE: Yes. NaGL. Capital N, small a, capital G, capital L.

VATA: Was it a name?

GRACE: Kind of. With a meaning. We considered it.

*She looks at* VATA, *then at* ROMAN *and finally at* MANOLO. *They sigh heavily.*

And it is still an option as far as I am concerned.

ROMAN *and* VATA *look at each other, then at* GRACE.

ROMAN & VATA: [*together*] You're not talking about me?

UNCLE CHUK *rings the bell.*

*Blackout.*

*End of Round Eight.*

*ROUND NINE*

UNCLE CHUK *holds up a call card: 'Round 9: NaGL again'.*

UNCLE CHUK: NaGL again. NaGL again. NaGL again.

*He shadowboxes.*

*He rings the bell.*

*The stage is in darkness.*

MANOLO*'s heavy breathing fills the space.*

*When the lights come up* ROMAN *and* VATA *are no longer there.*

MANOLO *lies on the couch panting heavily. He holds his right hand to his heart.* GRACE *bends over him.*

GRACE: How are you now?
MANOLO: I'm better.
GRACE: You look worse.

MANOLO *sits up and screams.*

MANOLO: But I feel better, you idiot!

*He falls back in pain, exhausted. It looks as if he is about to pass out.*

GRACE: Who knows, maybe they are right!
MANOLO: It is your fault—you shouldn't bring up that NaGL name… [*He hisses with pain.*] Right about what?

GRACE *goes to sit down next to* MANOLO.

GRACE: The divorce—divorce saved so many families.

MANOLO *twists in pain.*

MANOLO: Aaaaa! Are you crazy, woman?
GRACE: Why not? It's always better for kids: two homes, two Christmas trees …
MANOLO: Aaaaa! Stop it!
GRACE: … double the gifts, holiday trips.
MANOLO: Not that, you fuckwit!
GRACE: What then?
MANOLO: You sit on my penis. You squashed it and it all went numb.

GRACE *gets up.*

GRACE: Oh, sorry! How does it feel now?

MANOLO *sighs with relief.*

MANOLO: Better.

GRACE: Good.
MANOLO: Not good. Better.
GRACE: That's good.

MANOLO *turns and twists in agony and anger.*

MANOLO: And don't you ever mention that NaGL business again.
GRACE: Yeah, right. Who'd think back then, that when that blonde bimbo of a bitch saw your summer shoes and socks she'd say: 'Not a good look'? You just wanted to prove her wrong, silly, and you tried to introduce a new trend in fashion, and you called it NaGL—Not a Good Look. It didn't take off really. And to tell you the truth, I still think it wasn't a good name for a fashion label. One tends to think it was bound to fail, don't you agree? For a child though: I liked NaGL. But you wanted Roman—so here we are—it's all about timing, right? Like a divorce.

MANOLO *is exhausted with* GRACE*'s chatter.*

MANOLO: But they cannot divorce!
GRACE: There you go. [*Pause.*] But—why?
MANOLO: They are brother and sister, for God's sake.
GRACE: [*shaking her head*] Don't mix God with our earthly matters. God has enough on his plate.
MANOLO: God made them siblings.
GRACE: What about your little contribution?

MANOLO *jumps in convulsion.*

MANOLO: Aaaaa!

GRACE *turns to go.*

GRACE: Exactly what I thought! So now, I will leave you with it for the time being. Think it over, if you please.

GRACE *exits.*

MANOLO: Aaaaaaaaaaaa!

UNCLE CHUK *rings the bell.*

*Blackout.*

*End of Round Nine.*

*ROUND TEN*

UNCLE CHUK *holds up a call card: 'Round 10: Alcohol helps to balance things'.*

UNCLE CHUK: Alcohol helps to balance things. Alcohol helps to balance things.

*He shadowboxes.*

*He rings the bell.*

GRACE: [*in darkness*] I have something for us.

*Lights up.*

*She hides something behind her back.* MANOLO *tries to reach for it but she doesn't let him. They giggle.* MANOLO *tries again, and again he cannot reach. He gets upset and turns his back on* GRACE. *She produces a bottle of green absinth and shakes it above his head.* MANOLO *turns and sees the bottle. He claps his hands.*

Let's have one!

MANOLO: One?

GRACE: One. Why?

MANOLO: One only puts you off balance. It's kind of unsettling.

GRACE: You're naughty! Okay, let's have two.

MANOLO: [*thinking*] Okay. You have two. I have four.

GRACE: How come?

MANOLO: 'Cause you're a woman, you idiot!

*He pulls out a worn-out pamphlet and puts it right in* GRACE*'s face.*

I got it at our doctor's. Read.

GRACE *takes the pamphlet.*

GRACE: Dr Underson?

MANOLO: Yes. Read, now.

GRACE: [*reading*] 'Women can safely have two standard drinks per night and men can have four standard drinks…'

MANOLO *tries to snatch the pamphlet.*

MANOLO: You see?

GRACE: That's not fair.

MANOLO: I know, but that's the way it is.

GRACE: I don't think I like Dr Underson anymore. I'm not going there anymore.

MANOLO *tries to snatch the pamphlet again.*

MANOLO: Give it back. It's my proof.

GRACE: Hang on! [*She reads.*] 'It is safe to drink within the above limits on bases, but it is recommended however to have at least two alcohol-free days per week.'

MANOLO: Only two alcohol-free days per week? You're telling me I could drink five days a week. Week in, week out!

GRACE: I'm not telling you anything. That awful Dr Underson of ours—he's telling you.

*She throws the pamphlet at him. He catches it. She hides the bottle behind the couch.*

MANOLO: So, I could have five times four equals twenty standard drinks per week, fifty-six weeks per year, which comes to a total of one thousand one hundred and twenty standard drinks per year. Wow! Wow! That's impressive!

*He jumps up for joy.*

GRACE: And I could only have half of it? That is disgusting.

MANOLO: Don't worry, darling.

*He kisses her.*

You're only a woman. What can't be… that can't be… right?

GRACE: It can be. I can drink more than you and I'll prove it! One day.

MANOLO: Wishful thinking.

*He thinks. He starts sobbing.*

GRACE: What now?

MANOLO: I've just realised that I wasted my life.

GRACE: How come?

MANOLO: Most of it anyway.

GRACE: Why is that?

MANOLO: I wasted most of my drinking days.

*He throws himself on the floor.*

GRACE: And how old are you?
MANOLO: Why?
GRACE: Why not?
MANOLO: No! Tell me 'why'.
GRACE: So, I can find out how many days you actually wasted.
MANOLO: Far too many.
GRACE: [*thinking*] Alright. Think of it that way: Every time, every day you didn't have a drink you saved a gold coin… right?
MANOLO: More than that.
GRACE: Okay. More than that. Two gold coins.

MANOLO *keeps looking at her as if hypnotised.*

MANOLO: And?
GRACE: And? Imagine how much you saved by not having all those drinks.

MANOLO *imagines.*

And?
MANOLO: What?
GRACE: How much, do you think?
MANOLO: At least as much as you did at all your Christmas sales shopping over all those years.
GRACE: Really?
MANOLO: Yeah. You saved a fortune when you bought all those things we didn't need for half price… But you saved the second half of the price, right? You saved a fortune then!

*They both think for a while.*

GRACE: If we put what I saved with what you saved…
MANOLO: … we must have a fortune by now.
GRACE: Yes. We are rich!
MANOLO: Yes, you're damn right about that. [*He thinks.*] Isn't that funny however how your (one) fortune plus my (one) fortune equals still one fortune of ours? Wouldn't be it better if there were two fortunes in case we lose one?
GRACE: Mathematics are still a bit of mystery to me.

MANOLO *gets up.*

MANOLO: Never mind. [*He bows.*] May I?

GRACE *takes her time.*

GRACE: I dunno. Yeah, alright. You may.

*She gets up. They are about to start dancing, when* MANOLO *remembers something.*

MANOLO: You said you had something for us.
GRACE: Did I?
MANOLO: Yes.
GRACE: What was it?
MANOLO: A drink.
GRACE: A drink what?
MANOLO: A shot, a schnaps… you know.
GRACE: I do. So what?

MANOLO *grabs her.*

MANOLO: Oh! Get us a drink, woman!
GRACE: Oh! Now you're talking. Of course!

MANOLO *let's her go. She reaches behind the couch.*

Oh! It's not here!

MANOLO *collapses to the ground.*

MANOLO: All those years of savings for nothing?

*He moans.*

GRACE: Wait a sec. Here it is. [*She smiles.*] I was only kidding.

MANOLO *raises his head.*

MANOLO: You're going to kill me one day, you hard fart, with your bloody sense of humour.
GRACE: I just thought we could save a bit more… [*She takes a swig.*] Cheers!

MANOLO *grabs the bottle from her and takes a swig.*

MANOLO: Cheers! Save for what?
GRACE: For the dark hour.
MANOLO: The dark hour? Give me a break.

*He passes the bottle to* GRACE *to take a swig and then grabs it back.*

I love this stuff. It's green and makes me feel kind of… absinth.

*She tries to snatch the bottle from him.*

Hey! There is not such a thing as dark hour. [ *He drinks more.*] And when it finally comes it's too late anyway.

*Blackout.*

Shit!

GRACE: I told you!

MANOLO: Okay. You win. Can we finish it now? After all, we were saving for it.

*The sound of slapping.*

Ouch! It hurts.

GRACE: Good. It makes me feel more… absinth… you know.

MANOLO: I know. More is always good.

UNCLE CHUK *rings the bell.*

*Blackout.*

*End of Round Ten.*

*ROUND ELEVEN*

UNCLE CHUK *holds up a call card: 'Round 11: It never hurts to tango a bit and nothing beats to clarify a tango beat'.*

UNCLE CHUK: It never hurts to tango a bit and nothing beats to clarify a tango beat.

*He shadowboxes.*

*He rings the bell.*

*Lights up.*

MANOLO *and* GRACE *stand there ready to dance. They start to tango in silence. They circle the stage once and come to a sudden stop.*

MANOLO *breaks off the stance, leaving* GRACE *frozen in her position. He runs to a record player and puts on an old vinyl record. It plays tango music. He runs back to her. They start to dance again but this time they cannot find the right rhythm and the right steps. They stop.* MANOLO *takes the record off the turntable. He passes it to* GRACE.

MANOLO: Give me another one.

GRACE *takes the record and examines it.*

GRACE: This is another one.
MANOLO: What?
GRACE: There is only one record. This one.

MANOLO *grabs the record and brings it to his eyes.*

MANOLO: I don't have my glasses. What does it say?

GRACE *reads.*

GRACE: Tango.
MANOLO: Tango… Tan-go. Sounds bloody suspicious. Yes, tan-go. Sounds bloody Chinese.
GRACE: Tim-Tam sounds Chinese. And bin-go sounds bloody Chinese, but did we ever dance bin-go, darling?

MANOLO *hesitates.*

MANOLO: Where is your bloody Lonely Planet guide book?
GRACE: You're damn bloody right! I'll look it up.

GRACE *ducks under the table and starts leafing through the book.*

MANOLO: And?
GRACE: Doesn't look good.
MANOLO: Holy shit! Don't say! [*Pause.*] Say that you nailed it.
GRACE: I'm afraid not.
MANOLO: Don't be afraid, for God's sake, I'm your man. Just nail it, woman.
GRACE: Here it is: tango. But it's not Chinese.
MANOLO: What then?

GRACE *reads with difficulty.*

GRACE: Ar-gen-tin-nian.
MANOLO: Ar-gen-tin-nian?

GRACE *reads again. This time she makes it sound even more Chinese.*

GRACE: Ar-gen-tin-nian.

MANOLO: Ar-gen-tin-nian. Sounds Chinese.

*They think.*

GRACE: Chinese. 'Chinese' sounds so…

*They look at each other.*

GRACE & MANOLO: [*together*] … so English.

*They hide under the table.*

MANOLO: Yes. Holy shit! It's all so confusing. And scary. [*He thinks.*] So where the hell are we?

GRACE: We are here.

MANOLO: Here, where, you smart ass idiot?

GRACE: Here.

MANOLO *snatches the book from her.*

MANOLO: Let me have a look. [*He looks at the open page.*] There is a drawing here. Some kind of a sketch, you fuckin' rotten tomato of a brain.

GRACE: Don't be so fuckin' macho! [*She bends over the book.*] Where is it?

MANOLO: Here. See? First to the left. The right follows. Then forward and then right again.

GRACE: Let me see. [*She examines the drawing.*] Oh, yeah. I got it. Funny it took you so long to work it out.

MANOLO *turns to* GRACE *and raises his fist.*

MANOLO: I go first, right?!

GRACE: First left.

MANOLO *shakes his fist.*

MANOLO: I lead.

GRACE: Right-oh! You lead. Remember: two steps ahead and then to the side.

*They get up and tango.*

MANOLO: It works. It bloody works!

GRACE: Brings on the old happy days.

*The phone rings. They stop dancing. The phone keeps ringing.* GRACE *makes a move towards it.*

UNCLE CHUK: Don't answer the phone!

UNCLE CHUK *rings the bell.*

*Blackout.*

*End of Round Eleven.*

*ROUND TWELVE*

UNCLE CHUK *holds up a call card: 'Round 12: Don't blame Uncle Chuk'.*

UNCLE CHUK: Don't blame Uncle Chuk. Don't blame Uncle Chuk. Don't blame Uncle Chuk.

*He shadowboxes.*

*He rings the bell.*

*He storms in.*

Yabba! Tidda! Stay where you are!

*The phone keeps ringing.* GRACE *looks to* MANOLO. MANOLO *looks to* UNCLE CHUK. UNCLE CHUK *shakes his head.*

Don't answer the phone.

*Blackout.*

*The phone stops ringing.*

MANOLO: Not again!

GRACE: What is it?

MANOLO: Isn't that obvious? The power cut. We must have left the heater on for too long.

UNCLE CHUK: No, it's not the heater. It's me. It always happens whenever I arrive, wherever I arrive, for whatever reason I arrive. It just happens.

GRACE: The power cuts?

*From now on the lights slowly fade in.*

UNCLE CHUK: Whatever—anything—I am to blame: for the power cuts and for the heartburns, for the landslides in Brasil and for the World Cup loss, for the tsunamis and for the droughts, for the fleas and shark attacks, for the Roman Empire and for the English cuisine, for the millennium bug and for the sore tooth of the leader of the nation, for the whale hunting and for the overpopulation of Japan…

GRACE: That's quite an impressive list. Are you sure you don't want to share some blame… anything… we're family, after all?

UNCLE CHUK: Family? Aboriginals? You? You have enough on your plate.

MANOLO: An example, please.

UNCLE CHUK: Well, your gunnadoos… *jarjums*… your kids, you know! And this upcoming divorce of yours. I don't blame, God forbid…

*The lights are back to normal now.* GRACE *and* MANOLO *look at each other.*

GRACE & MANOLO: [*together*] Whose divorce?

UNCLE CHUK: Oh, no. You don't know, yet. It's my fault again!

*The phone rings.*

Don't worry about the phone.

MANOLO: Why?

UNCLE CHUK: It's me.

MANOLO: What do you mean?

UNCLE CHUK: Don't answer. It's me calling you, but since I'm here, there's no need to answer.

GRACE: Hang on: Why would you call us if you're already here with us?

UNCLE CHUK: That's my point: Why would you need to answer?

MANOLO: My home is my castle!

MANOLO *throws himself across the room to pick up the phone.*

*Gong!*

*Lights down.*

END OF FIRST STANZA

## SECOND STANZA

---

*Darkness.*

MANOLO: Yep… Yep… Mhmmm… Yep. Okay. Will do… Yep.

*The sound of a receiver being put down is heard, followed by an engaged signal. Silence.*

GRACE: And?

*Pause.*

MANOLO: Nothing. [*Pause.*] It was him.
UNCLE CHUK: I told you. It's all my fault.

*He starts crying. The sound of his heavy footsteps getting further and further away are followed by the sound of a slamming door. Silence.*

GRACE & MANOLO: [*together*] He told us.

*End of Round Twelve.*

*Lights up.*

*ROUND THIRTEEN*

UNCLE CHUK *holds up a call card: 'Round 13: Gratitude always makes people stand up'.*

UNCLE CHUK: Gratitude always makes people stand up. Gratitude always makes people stand up.

*He shadowboxes.*

*He rings the bell.*

GRACE *and* MANOLO *sit on the couch.* ROMAN *keeps pacing up and down in front of them with his eyes glued to the floor.* VATA *sits across the stage from* MANOLO. GRACE *is watching them intensely.*

ROMAN: One of the major reasons for all our divorce-ive actions is your extreme lack of gratitude, which…

GRACE *and* MANOLO *jump to their feet.* ROMAN *stops and looks up.* VATA *is furious.*

VATA: *Alla Direzione dell'Hotel Locarno!* Roman!

ROMAN: *Riservata mio! Scheisse!* Why do you get up?

MANOLO *and* GRACE *look at each other.* GRACE *pokes* MANOLO.

MANOLO: You said: 'Gratitude'.

ROMAN: Yes: 'Of gratitude'.

VATA *rolls her eyes and growls.* ROMAN *looks at* VATA *frightened.*

Right. Okay. I said: 'Lack of gratitude'.

GRACE: Did you, Roman?

ROMAN *jumps and stomps his feet.*

ROMAN: Don't! Don't call me that. I'm not fucking Roman. For you, I'm fucking Polish, if at all.

GRACE: But she just called you Roman!

ROMAN: Aaaa! Why did *you* call me that in the first place?

GRACE: [*pointing to* MANOLO] It was his idea.

ROMAN *and* VATA *turn to* MANOLO.

MANOLO: I thought you were Italian.

VATA: … Fucking Italian?

MANOLO: No. Bloody Italian.

GRACE: Bloody Italian?

MANOLO: *Si*. I thought that since I am a bloody Italian, that you… you know.

*He shrugs his shoulders and circles his arms.* ROMAN *looks at him and shrugs his shoulders, then circles his arms.*

ROMAN: No. I don't.

GRACE & MANOLO: [*together*] Well…

*They shrug their shoulders, circle their arms and sit down.*

VATA: And what about me?

GRACE: Oh, that's a completely different case. Vata is a new English name.

VATA: Bloody English?

GRACE: No. [*She thinks.*] Fuckin' English. [*Pause.*] You see, it was to show our gratitude…

MANOLO *and* GRACE *stand up.*

... to express the joy with certain authorities and their bloody ideas. VATA—spelled with all capital letters, as you know... as we all know... very bloody unique, one may, bloody, say... V.A.T.A. Stands for: Value Added Tax Appreciated. In short VATA.

VATA: Vaaaataaa! It sounds fuckin' Italian.

GRACE: Yes. Good point. And it sounds bloody Polish, too. It means 'cotton wool'.

VATA: [*shaking her head furiously*] No fuckin' Polish. Bloody Italian! Bloody: *RiserVATA*, *honoRATA*, *captiVATA*, *cippoLATA*, *mamma mia! DolceVATA...*

ROMAN: What did you say?

VATA *freezes. She looks at* ROMAN.

VATA: *DolceVATA!*

ROMAN: *La dolce vita!*

VATA: *Silenzio!* No *'La'! Nome! Cognome! Indirizzo! Telefono! Grazia!*

GRACE *bends over to* MANOLO.

GRACE: I love it when she gets bloody upset. She sounds so cultured and so bloody continental.

VATA: *La votra opinione e importante!*

GRACE: What does it mean, darling?

VATA *growls.*

VATA: I have no bloody idea. It just rolls out of me when I'm bloody upset.

MANOLO: 'Your opinion is important to us.'

ROMAN: And it'd better be.

MANOLO: No. It's what she said.

ROMAN *thinks.*

ROMAN: So you say.

MANOLO *hides behind* GRACE.

MANOLO: So she says.

MANOLO *points to* VATA. VATA *looks to* ROMAN.

VATA: Are you bloody Italian?

MANOLO: Yes. I mean: No. A bit of all.

ROMAN: So what does all this make of me to be?

GRACE *and* MANOLO *squat behind the couch.*

GRACE & MANOLO: [*together*] You are…

*They hesitate.*

ROMAN *cuts in.*

ROMAN: Not fuckin' American?
GRACE & MANOLO: [*together*] … fuckin' Australian maybe?
ROMAN: Maybe? Extreme lack of gratitiude, you two!

MANOLO *and* GRACE *get up.* VATA *and* ROMAN *growl.* GRACE *and* MANOLO *sit on the couch.*

VATA: Where were we?

ROMAN *resumes pacing up and down.*

ROMAN: Where were we? Anyone?

MANOLO *and* GRACE *shake their heads.*

Yes… Right… Wellllll…
UNCLE CHUK: [*prompting*] One of the major…
ROMAN: Enough! [*Pause.*] One of the major reasons for our decision is your extreme lack of gratitude…

MANOLO *and* GRACE *try to resist getting up, but nevertheless start to ascend.* ROMAN *turns to them and continues talking, without taking his eyes off them. They descend slowly to the couch.*

… lack of gratitude pushed to extremes. I work my guts out, and for what?
VATA: [*prompting*] Show them. C'mon.

ROMAN *lifts his shirt and shows them his belly button.*

No. Not this. Show them your arm. The veins.

ROMAN *thinks, then rolls up his left sleeve.*

No. The other one. You have big, good bloody veins on your right arm.

ROMAN *rolls up his right sleeve and is surprised to reveal a mesh of blue-coloured, thick veins drawn up on his arm. He looks at it and slowly smiles—proud and pleased.* VATA *nods.*

ROMAN: You see?

*GRACE and MANOLO close their eyes.*

MANOLO: I can't watch. Even a bare thought of a cardiac system pumping blood through man's unworthy bloody body makes me faint. I said too much, already.

*He faints. GRACE attends to him by slapping him on his cheeks. MANOLO opens his eyes.*

VATA: There you are! He works his guts out and all you can do in return is to faint. You're not worth it. It is not worth it.

ROMAN: Not at all.

VATA: So we decided to divorce.

*MANOLO and GRACE jump up and freeze. After a while they start wailing out of control.*

I knew they couldn't take it with dignity, like men.

*They exit. MANOLO and GRACE stop crying.*

ROMAN & VATA: [*together, offstage*] And stop crying!

*MANOLO and GRACE look at each other.*

GRACE: They don't know.

MANOLO: No. Not at all. [*He runs to close both doors.*] I'll show you gratitude.

*He squats and gets tense. He produces a big fart.*

GRACE: You're a swine!

*They both burst out laughing. Silence.*

How are you now, honey?

MANOLO: I'm definitely better now.

*UNCLE CHUK rings the bell.*

*Blackout.*

*End of Round Thirteen.*

*ROUND FOURTEEN*

*UNCLE CHUK holds up a call card: 'Round 14: Lonely Planet guide to divorce'.*

UNCLE CHUK: Lonely Planet guide to divorce. Lonely Planet guide to divorce.

*He shadowboxes.*

*He rings the bell.*

MANOLO: Got it?

GRACE: Got a book.

MANOLO: And?

GRACE: Can't see a bloody thing.

*Lights up.*

MANOLO *grabs the book from* GRACE.

MANOLO: Let me have a look. [*He examines the book. He opens it and brings it to his eyes.*] Can't find my bloody glasses. You read it.

*He hands the book back to her. She leafs through the pages.*

GRACE: Well… Where do I start? [*She closes the book and looks at the cover.*] Okay. Here. [*She reads with difficulty.*] *Step-by-Step Illustrated Lonely Planet Guide to Divorce*? Oh, no. Hang on… *Lonely Planet Guide Through Divorce*? I'm not sure, actually. It's faded a fair bit. Must be read often.

MANOLO: What's the difference: 'to' or 'through'? It's a good title, either way. Go on!

GRACE: [*shaking her head*] Well… I don't know. It's a big difference. You say 'to', before you get there: 'guide *to* divorce'. And you say 'through', once you are there already and you need directions, help… Right?

MANOLO: Alright. I'll go with 'to'. 'To divorce'. 'Through' sounds bloody scary. Sounds bloody American actually.

GRACE: Funny you mention that. By the way: have you noticed that nothing sounds bloody Russian these days—

MANOLO: [*thinking*] 'Putin' sounds Russian.

GRACE: [*thinking*] Doesn't strike me… as such. Sounds rather naughty to me. Never mind. Love you, honey. 'To' is the right choice. 'To' is much better. Right. Family always first. Then some stupid 'divorce', right?

MANOLO *drops to the ground and his body twists in convulsion.*

Is everything okay?

MANOLO *gestures her to be quiet and continues his spasms on the floor. Suddenly his antics come to a stop.*

MANOLO: I had to get it out of my system.

GRACE: I understand. And how do you feel now, honey?

MANOLO *gets up.*

MANOLO: I'm better. I think.

GRACE: You know, it's interesting: You've been better quite a few times lately. You've been better for the last three weeks or more, but you haven't been good… You are not good, are you?

MANOLO: No, I'm not. Not good, yet.

GRACE: And that's my point. How long can you be better without actually being *good*?

MANOLO: It's interesting, yes. It's more of a linguistic problem, really…

GRACE: It's more of a philosophical problem, rather…

*They think.*

MANOLO: Yes. Philosophical rather or ethical, because, when I say I'm good, I am bad, actually. Not good at all.

GRACE: Not good at all. You're a bad boy, Manolo. That's what I mean. And that could be quite a good reason for…

*She indicates the book. He drops to the ground.*

MANOLO: Don't even mention it. I want it out of my system, and I can feel it's back… it's still there…

MANOLO *burps.*

GRACE: Is it gone now, Manolo?

MANOLO: No! I just burped, you damned shadow of a creature. And, please, stop calling me Manolo, right!

GRACE: That's your name.

MANOLO: And yours is Grace. So what? Look at me—I am somebody else. And when I look at you, I see somebody else. We are not the same. Not anymore.

*He lies motionless, exhausted.*

GRACE: Silly talk, honey. I can see now that you're better again. Get up and forget about this all… guide… Lonely Planet… this… situation, you know.

MANOLO *doesn't move.* GRACE *shoves the book under the table and lies back next to him. She takes a deep breath.*

Okay, ready? One, two, three: Gratitude.

*They both get up.*

UNCLE CHUK *rings the bell.*

*Blackout.*

*End of Round Fourteen.*

*The phone rings and continues ringing into the next scene.*

## *ROUND FIFTEEN*

UNCLE CHUK *holds up a call card: 'Round 15: It's me. Uncle Chuk again.'*

UNCLE CHUK: It's me. Uncle Chuk again. It's me. Uncle Chuk again.

*He shadowboxes.*

*He rings the bell.*

It's me. Uncle Chuk.

*The door (stage left) opens and the light spills in.* UNCLE CHUK *stands in the door.*

MANOLO: Never heard of Uncle Chuk. Have you, darling?
GRACE: No, never.
UNCLE CHUK: I don't blame you. Who would? But don't blame me for your own shortcomings and for your own children especially. I don't blame you for my legs lost in combat, for my foul tongue, do I? I don't blame you for my broken arms and poked eyes, do I? I don't see you guilty of drilling a hole through my heart and singing a lullaby in the middle of my childhood day.

MANOLO *and* GRACE *slowly creep up towards the open door.*

And I don't blame you for putting my bloodied head on a giant fork for no reason at all in the memorable summer of the 1944—no, I don't. But I cannot help myself and say what I see with my ever-open eyes. So I'm telling you: There's no need for any divorce, yet. Please! Stick together, you shameless people. It's by far too early for a big void…

MANOLO *and* GRACE *close the door. It's pitch dark again.*

[*Offstage*] … too early, please… too early for the ultimate solitude…

GRACE & MANOLO: [*together*] Shut the fuck up!

UNCLE CHUK: [*offstage*] No. Don't put the blame on yourselves. It's me! Uncle Chuk. I'm sorry for what I see but I can't close my eyes. Ever.

GRACE: Then shut your bloody mouth!

UNCLE CHUK: Okay. Done. [*Pause.*] Love you, people!

*The phone stops ringing. Silence. After a brief moment:*

*Shuffling feet.* GRACE *is moving.*

MANOLO: Shush!

*Silence. Lights up.*

GRACE *gestures to* MANOLO. *She spreads her arms wide and shrugs her shoulders and mouths a soundless: 'What?'*

Shut up, will you?

GRACE *freezes. They listen.*

*Silence.*

Did you hear that?

GRACE: What?

MANOLO: Anything?

GRACE: Did I hear anything?

MANOLO: Yes. Anything. Something?

GRACE: [*thinking*] No. I didn't.

MANOLO: Didn't you?

GRACE: No, I didn't. I told you.

MANOLO: Shush!

*They both listen.*

*Silence.*

GRACE: Did *you* hear anything?

MANOLO: Just then?

GRACE: Yes?

MANOLO: No.

GRACE: So, what was it then?

MANOLO: A telephone.

GRACE: A telephone?
MANOLO: Yes. A telephone. I thought someone called us.

GRACE *sighs dreamily and closes her eyes.*

GRACE: Wouldn't that be wonderful? Imagine: someone calling us.
MANOLO: I wonder who could that be?
GRACE: It could be a Sunday Lotto office.
MANOLO: Why would they call us?
GRACE: To let us know that we won! That we are millionaires.
MANOLO: That'd be something. I wonder why didn't they call?

GRACE *nods in agreement.*

GRACE: Yes. Why?

*They sit in silence.*

Manolo?

MANOLO *gives her a look.*

Sorry. I forgot. [*Pause.*] Hey, you!
MANOLO: Yes?
GRACE: Would you like to buy a lottery ticket? [*Pause.*] I have one.
MANOLO: So keep it!
GRACE: No… I'd rather sell it.
MANOLO: Why? You've had it for a long time. Why would you like to get rid of it now?
GRACE: I don't know. Some need for change in my life, I believe. I've had it since we met.
MANOLO: [*thinking*] Hang on. Maybe it's out of date.
GRACE: How can 'Your Lucky Ticket That Will Change Your Life For Ever' be out of date before it changes your life?
MANOLO: Yeah. You're right.
GRACE: Hang on. Shush! You heard something?
MANOLO: You heard it, too! Right?
GRACE: I think so.

*Lights up.*

UNCLE CHUK *rings the bell.*

*Blackout.*

*End of Round Fifteen.*

*ROUND SIXTEEN*

UNCLE CHUK *holds up a call card: 'Round 16: Theory comes in handy only when you practise'.*

UNCLE CHUK: Theory comes in handy only when you practise. Theory comes in handy only when you practise.

*He shadowboxes.*

*He rings the bell.*

MANOLO *and* GRACE *sit opposite each other at the table.* ROMAN *and* VATA *sit behind the table, facing the audience.*

VATA: What did you hear?
GRACE: A phone…? Maybe?
MANOLO: Yes. A phone, I think.

ROMAN *and* VATA *listen.*

ROMAN: I hear nothing.
VATA: No, nothing. [*She remembers something and slams her forehead.*] You two. You don't have a phone, do you?
MANOLO: Don't we?
GRACE: No. We don't.

*She looks at* MANOLO.

MANOLO: Yes… We don't.

VATA *slams her fist on the table.*

VATA: Then, don't play games on us. We're trying to get you through a divorce procedure.
ROMAN: We're trying to make it easier for all of us. And you… [*Pause.*] What do you have to offer?
GRACE: Maybe you'd like a lottery ticket? I have one. You never know. It could be the winner!
ROMAN: Is it the same one which you tried to sell to Vata last time?
GRACE: This time it is for free.
VATA: You have this ticket ever since I remember. C'mon! Beat it, you old bum!
GRACE: It hasn't won anything, yet!

VATA: And it never will. Isn't it obvious, you loser? It's well passed its use-by date.

GRACE: So what? It's a winning ticket. I asked for a winning ticket, when I bought it.

ROMAN: Oh, you're stupid… And hopeless.

GRACE *starts sobbing.* MANOLO *gets up.*

MANOLO: Let me point out to you that you're wrong, young man. [*He clears his throat.*] Quite opposite. [*He turns to* GRACE.] You are full of hope… And ever so bloody optimistic. Especially when it comes down to your children. You always had faith in them.

ROMAN & VATA: [*together*] Oh, not again!

MANOLO: Oh, yes—many more times, if you, please! Now get up and apologise to your Mamma and Papa! 'Hopeless'! I'll show you hopeless!

*He grabs* GRACE *and forces her up.* ROMAN *and* VATA *look at each other.*

ROMAN: In theory we're doing fine.

VATA: Fuck your theory. We need more practice!

MANOLO *raises his fist as if to strike* GRACE. ROMAN *and* VATA *jump to their feet.*

ROMAN & VATA: [*together*] Okay, okay. We apologise, Mamma.

*They sit down.* MANOLO *raises his fist at* GRACE *again.*

MANOLO: And Pappa?

VATA *and* ROMAN *jump to their feet again.*

ROMAN & VATA: [*together*] And Papa.

*They all sit down.* GRACE *stops sobbing.*

GRACE: See what you do to us? Go now. And don't you ever try to guide us anymore through any-bloody-thing.

MANOLO, VATA & ROMAN: [*together*] Amen.

UNCLE CHUK *rings the bell.*

*Blackout.*

*End of Round Sixteen.*

*ROUND SEVENTEEN*

UNCLE CHUK *holds up a call card: 'Round 17: Inside out and outside in—that other creature looking at me—a few personal reflections on the subject of life theatre and mirror'.*

UNCLE CHUK: Inside out and outside in—that other creature looking at me—a few personal reflections on the subject of life theatre and mirror.

*He shadowboxes.*

*He rings the bell.*

*Lights up.*

ROMAN *and* VATA *are gone.* GRACE *stands in the centre holding a mirror in front of her. Her face twists in a succession of angry, furious, upset, confused and plain stupid facial expressions.* MANOLO *observes her.*

MANOLO: Un-bloody-believable!

GRACE *starts crying.* MANOLO *runs to her and takes her in his arms.*

What happened?

GRACE: I don't like it.

MANOLO: The mirror?

GRACE: No. That creature.

MANOLO: What creature?

GRACE: That creature, which lives in the mirror.

MANOLO: There could be no creature living in the mirror. The mirror is there for reflecting reality… life…

GRACE: My grandma used to say that theatre mirrors life.

MANOLO: Has she ever been to live theatre?

GRACE: I don't think so.

MANOLO: People get confused, you see… My grand-grandpa used to say that theatre was to caricature people in order to make the points clear, but I don't think he had ever been to live theatre either. But the thing is that your grandma and my grand-grandpa passed their valuable knowledge down to the next generations of… of us… And we can pass it on too. So family is good, after all. If only to pass on the family knowledge, so we don't have to make the same mistakes over and over again, so we don't have to go to live theatre, for example, to see it mirror life—we can use mirrors instead.

GRACE *stops sobbing.*

GRACE: But our mirror stopped doing its job properly some time ago. [*She thinks.*] Since Sunday. January the twenty-sixth, when we came back from our last holidays?

MANOLO: We went for holidays once only, didn't we?

GRACE: Yes. Wasn't that lovely?

*They think.*

That was twenty-one years ago today. And it feels like yesterday.

MANOLO: It was yesterday… if you know what I mean.

GRACE: I don't.

*Pause.*

MANOLO: It was after we retired. Our first holiday.

GRACE: Do you remember now?

MANOLO: Yes.

GRACE: What did we retire from?

MANOLO: I don't think that we retired 'from' anything. We retired 'into'…

GRACE: Retired from nothing?

MANOLO: Yes. That's right: from nothing into being retired. Into being pensioners.

GRACE: I remember the smell.

MANOLO: The smell of burning bushes.

GRACE: The smell of ashes.

MANOLO: Yes. It was hot.

GRACE: … That other creature lives there ever since.

MANOLO: What creature?

GRACE: The mirror monster.

MANOLO: You're talking sheer bullshit!

GRACE: I'm not. If you only looked in once, you'd see it for yourself.

MANOLO: I'm not doing any girly, stupid, sissy activities.

GRACE *starts crying.*

GRACE: You're afraid of the monster.

MANOLO: I'm not afraid of something which is not even there.

GRACE *stops crying and stomps her foot.*

GRACE: It is there!
MANOLO: How d'you know?

GRACE *grabs a framed wedding photo from the wall. She holds it up for* MANOLO *to see.*

GRACE: I know what I look like. I have a proof here.

MANOLO *looks at the picture and at* GRACE. *He snatches the photograph. Then he looks closer at it. And then he looks at her again.*

MANOLO: Can you describe that monster to me?
GRACE: It's old and ugly… and horrible.

MANOLO *thinks. Then he grabs the mirror and puts it in front of* GRACE. *She screams in terror.*

Aaaaaa!

*She snaps the mirror from him and places it in front of his face.* MANOLO *looks in and jumps in horror.*

MANOLO: Oooooo!
GRACE: You see.

MANOLO *forces the mirror around to her face. She jumps.*

Noooo!

*She struggles to turn the mirror to face* MANOLO.

MANOLO: Oooooo! I don't like this monster.

*They struggle. The mirror falls down, but doesn't break. They look down at it.*

Good.
GRACE: Facedown.
MANOLO: It's trapped.
GRACE: They say: If a mirror falls and doesn't break, there'll be no love for seven years for the person who dropped it.

*She keeps sobbing.*

MANOLO: [*thinking*] Did *you* drop it?

GRACE: *We* dropped it.

MANOLO: We'll leave it where it is. [*Pause.*] Where do they say that?

GRACE: In some of those far-off countries.

*Pause.*

MANOLO: We are not in a far-off country.

GRACE: Aren't we?

MANOLO: [*shrugging his shoulders*] I don't know actually. Where did you hear it?

GRACE: Not that far from here. [*Pause.*] Somewhere here actually.

MANOLO: There you go… actually.

GRACE: Seven years! And I like seven! Seven days of a week… Seven deadly sins: PrideEnvyAngerAvariceSadnessGluttonyLust… and on the seventh day rested.

MANOLO: We'll leave it where it is. Facedown.

GRACE: What about love?

MANOLO: What about it?

GRACE: I cannot imagine living without love for seven long years.

MANOLO: What about seven short years? Would that change anything?

GRACE: I don't know. [*Pause.*] It's just that I cannot *imagine*… life without love. It's about *imagination*, not about *love*, you idiot.

*She cries.*

UNCLE CHUK *rings the bell.*

*Blackout.*

*End of Round Seventeen.*

## *ROUND EIGHTEEN*

UNCLE CHUK *holds up a call card: 'Round 18: Sing your praise to the Lord—we are all one here… in a sense'.*

UNCLE CHUK: Sing your praise to the Lord—we are all one here… in a sense. Sing your praise to the Lord—we are all one here… in a sense.

*He shadowboxes.*

*He rings the bell.*

GRACE *sings in darkness.*

GRACE: [*soprano voice*] We remember, oh o'r Lord,
How you loved, oh all of us,
There was place for everyone
In your heart, oh in your heart,
For those good and for those bad,
Only willing to accept—
Even sinner lives in hope
Of meeting you almighty Lord.

*She clears her throat.*

Hmmm. It doesn't make much sense, really.

MANOLO: No, it doesn't. Yet you sing it.

*Lights up.*

GRACE: What matters is the singing, the pure pleasure of it. It is like a prayer going directly to… I don't know. To heaven? Maybe. [*Pause.*] I often wonder what made me join the Filipino choir and I come to the conclusion that it was my way to emphasise the uniqueness of that choir. Yes, by being not Filipino and by being much taller than all the other members of the choir, I seemed to point even stronger towards the Filipino-choirness of our Filipino choir, and yet making them feeling more like us. Yes, by being one with them I allowed them for being one with me, with us, I mean. Because we are all one here. We are—

MANOLO: Oh, shut up. It sounds like *Paradise Now* and free love for all—and all that hippie stuff.

GRACE: Is that what you think?

MANOLO: No, not really. I didn't mean that. It's just that it always puzzled me why you joined it in the first place, before you realised that you emphasise the Filipino-choirness of the Filipino choir by being different.

GRACE: Maybe I was a Filipino in my previous life?

MANOLO: Hmmm… On my part, I only let you join this choir because you always have orgasms after the practice.

GRACE: If you want me to resign, I'll resign.

MANOLO: [*thinking*] Did you fake any orgasms?

GRACE: Why would I?

MANOLO: In order to keep me happy with your Filipino-choirness, maybe?

GRACE: [*thinking*] And did you?

MANOLO *looks at* GRACE *and thinks.*

MANOLO: And what if I did?

GRACE *looks at* MANOLO *and thinks.*

GRACE: Nothing.
MANOLO: Okay. I didn't.
GRACE: Neither did I.

*Pause.*

MANOLO *looks at* GRACE.

MANOLO: Maybe one…
GRACE: One?!
MANOLO: Two… maybe.
GRACE: But why?
MANOLO: To check if I'm not gay.
GRACE: And?
MANOLO: No. I'm not.

GRACE *approaches him and looks him straight in the eyes.*

GRACE: Two?
MANOLO: Three… four maybe?
GRACE: Why so many, if you're not gay?
MANOLO: Just to make absolutely sure, you see. Because if I was gay it could be a good reason…
GRACE: Reason for what?
MANOLO: [*thinking*] And what about you?

GRACE *jumps back.*

GRACE: I'm not gay!

MANOLO *confronts her now with a hard look.*

Maybe just a little bit… not much gay.

MANOLO *jumps in fury.*

MANOLO: See! Why do you tell me that you're gay, now? What makes you think that?
GRACE: I faked some orgasms too. That's why.
MANOLO: Oh, my God! Did you? I will never get an erection again. [*He freezes.*] How many?

GRACE: How many what?
MANOLO: Fake orgasms, you bloody idiot.
GRACE: One.
MANOLO: One?
GRACE: One. Yes. [*She remembers.*] One, I'm sure.

MANOLO *looks her square in the eyes.*

MANOLO: Which one?
GRACE: After the Filipino choir.
MANOLO: Oh, my God!
GRACE: What?
MANOLO: I have an erection.
GRACE: Congratulations.

MANOLO *freezes.*

MANOLO: It doesn't make sense.
GRACE: No. It doesn't. Do you still have it?
MANOLO: Yes. Unbelievable. Do something! It hurts.
GRACE: Okay. Okay… Think shopping.

MANOLO *closes his eyes and opens after a short moment.*

MANOLO: Gone. That was bloody hot.
GRACE: Close shave.
MANOLO: Nearly got me a heart attack. You are something, you know. Something special, you bloody idiot of a woman.
GRACE: I know I am.
MANOLO: Love you, sheep poo.
GRACE: Love you, elephant piss.

*They hug.*

MANOLO *smiles.*

MANOLO: Life is beautiful.
GRACE: You're a dickhead.
MANOLO: Yes, I know. But it was good, hey?
GRACE: Hey.

*They sit down and stare ahead.*

MANOLO: After our wedding, remember?
GRACE: Yes?

MANOLO: Was it a pyjama party or a dress-up party?
GRACE: All I remember was a hard labour party ever since.
MANOLO: They don't differ, the parties, do they? No matter what you call them it's always about making lots of noise and having a ball with your pals without much consideration to others.
GRACE: And you always wake up the next day with a monstrous hangover… and with your hand in a smelly potty.

UNCLE CHUK *rings the bell.*

*Blackout.*

*End of Round Eighteen.*

*ROUND NINETEEN*

UNCLE CHUK *holds up a call card: 'Round 19: We never forget things we never remembered'.*

UNCLE CHUK: We never forget things we never remembered. We never forget things we never remembered.

*He shadowboxes.*

*He rings the bell.*

*Loud stomping is heard in the darkness, followed by furious jumping on the spot.*

*Lights up.*

VATA: How could you forget?
GRACE: I don't know!

GRACE *starts crying.*

ROMAN: Shut up, you old fart! [*He turns to* MANOLO.] What about you?
MANOLO: I didn't forget.
ROMAN: Far out! You surprise me sometimes!
VATA: Where are the fuckin' flowers, then?
MANOLO: What flowers?
VATA: The flowers for my B-day, you old prick!
MANOLO: I forgot, I think.
VATA: There you go!
ROMAN: Tricky, cheeky old bastard, hey?

*He laughs and shakes his head. Then without warning he charges towards* MANOLO.

MANOLO: Now I remember: I didn't forget. I simply never remember any fucking birthdays and anniversaries, so how could I forget something that I never remembered in the first place?

ROMAN: This makes sense. [*He turns to* VATA.] We'll put it on the list: 'Never remembers important family dates'. What do you think?

VATA: I think it's not good enough. And at least *she* could make an effort.

GRACE: We made an effort. It's not bloody easy, you see, because your birthday kept shifting, with Easter, you know—every bloody year, a different date. Impossible to follow. Sometimes in April, sometimes in March. It's just one of those 'moving dates'—like 'moving sands': here today, there tomorrow. And we are simple people, you know…

ROMAN: This makes bloody sense, too… But what about my B-day? I was born in summer.

MANOLO: In winter, you idiot.

ROMAN: In summer, you dickhead.

MANOLO: Don't you tell me, because I was there and I remember well! You were born under a Christmas tree.

ROMAN: You see: summer!

GRACE *bends over to* MANOLO*'s ear.*

GRACE: [*whispering*] For them it is summer, you bum-bum. Turkey on the beach, blah-blah-blah, Christmas party before, New Year barbeque afterwards. For us it's winter: snow, howling winds, blistering cold, carols at midnight in a crowded church…

MANOLO: I forgot. You're right. Bloody hell. [*He turns to* ROMAN.] So you were born in summer. You see? We remember.

ROMAN: So why won't you ever buy me flowers for my B-day?

MANOLO: [*thinking*] Because you're a boy.

ROMAN: So what? What's wrong with being a boy?

MANOLO: To be honest, it's the same thing as with Easter, you see. You were born on the Christmas Day and I remember it was Friday, because on Fridays we always have a bottle of blood-red wine and after that we always have little… you know…

ROMAN & VATA: [*together*] Gross! Don't say it, we bloody well know what you did on Friday nights, you dirty old people.

MANOLO *and* GRACE *giggle.*

MANOLO: There you go. Where were we? Aha—that Christmas Friday, we didn't… you know…

GRACE: Well, we did, actually, but we couldn't finish, because you were in such a hurry.

ROMAN & VATA: [*together*] Oh, yuck!

MANOLO: Yeah! And the next bloody Christmas comes and it's bloody Saturday. And the next it's Monday. So, you see how we got confused. At least one can say that you always get some kind of celebrations.

GRACE: And a gift. Every year.

MANOLO: Year in. Year out.

GRACE *and* MANOLO *hug each other.*

GRACE: That was bloody good, man. It brings on memories.

MANOLO: Yes, it does. I haven't had an erection in a long time.

GRACE: Neither have I. I actually don't remember having one at all, and you, on the contrary, I can remember you always saying, 'Come over, woman, I have an erection'.

VATA: Boys have it better: a gift every bloody year, an erection, a Christmas tree and a bucks' party.

GRACE: We have our hen nights, babes.

VATA *starts crying.*

VATA: That's right. And that's all, smelly pants! How does it sound in comparison to an erection act, for example? It's not right. And it's not my fault.

UNCLE CHUK: [*offstage*] It's my fault most likely!

MANOLO, GRACE & ROMAN: [*together*] Oh, shut up, Uncle Chuk!

VATA: I want a divorce.

*She cries louder.* MANOLO, GRACE *and* ROMAN *look at her in confusion.*

GRACE: Who do you want to divorce, then?

VATA: You!

GRACE: You can't divorce me. I'm your family.

VATA *stops sobbing. They all sit in silence.*

I was so scared that you'd be born bloody black.

MANOLO: Why, for fuck's sake?

ROMAN: Are you racist?

GRACE: No, God forbid. I love black, darling. You seem blackish in this light to me and I love you, after all.

VATA: What would be the problem with me being black, then?

GRACE: If you were born black it would be a good cause for a divorce.

ROMAN: How come?

GRACE: I don't bloody know. In those ancient days, people were so behind our times.

MANOLO: And so superstitious. Dark Ages!

GRACE: Wasn't it wrong, darling?

MANOLO: Yes, that's right. If Vata was born black I'd divorce you on the bloody spot—if I only could.

VATA: If you only could. But you didn't divorce her when I was born, right?!

MANOLO: No. One had to get married first in those days if one wanted to divorce.

GRACE: How banal.

MANOLO: And complicated.

GRACE: Life is much easier nowdays.

MANOLO: Yeah. Straightforward.

GRACE *gives* MANOLO *a 'high five'.*

VATA *looks at them, disgusted.*

VATA: I hate your guts, old farts. [*She turns to* MANOLO.] We have to consider our options now.

ROMAN: This is a fantastic idea!

VATA: Shut up, you pea brain! This is what we'll do: We need a divorce in order to improve the quality of our life and lives of all those involved and concerned with our state's wellbeing. We'll go to the States, to Vegas, to be precise, and we'll get a divorce, because if they can marry anyone in Vegas, they can give a divorce to anyone. We will start a new life there by: helping people in general, starting careers of sorts for ourselves, at the same time we'll both become perfect housewives and either I'll obtain my own right to my own erection or you'll give up your right to your erection. Alternatively, you'll share yours with me. Equally! [*She turns to* MANOLO *and* GRACE.] We don't need you anymore, losers!

*She turns to* ROMAN.

ROMAN: I love you, honey bunny. I want to marry you…
VATA: Oh, just be silent and follow me…

VATA *storms out.*

ROMAN: … just to divorce you, if you know what I mean!

ROMAN *runs after her.* MANOLO *looks after them.*

*Blackout.*

UNCLE CHUK *rings the bell.*

*End of Round Nineteen.*

*ROUND TWENTY*

UNCLE CHUK *holds up a call card: 'Round 20: Curiosity'.*

*He says nothing.*

*He rings the bell.*

*Lights up.*

GRACE *goes to close the door.*

GRACE: If only they listened till we tell them the whole story.
MANOLO: What is the whole story?
GRACE: That we got married for our tenth anniversary.
MANOLO: Did we? Why?
GRACE: No idea. Some kind of one-off financial benefit from the state, maybe?
MANOLO: Possible. [*He thinks.*] Technically we can get a divorce, then. Do you know if there is any one-off payment from the state in case people divorce?
GRACE: Why do you ask?
MANOLO: Curiosity, I think.

GRACE *starts crying.*

GRACE: I hate it when you're curious.

UNCLE CHUK *rings the bell.*

*Blackout.*

*End of Round Twenty.*

*ROUND TWENTY-ONE*

*The stage is in darkness.*

UNCLE CHUK: Round twenty-one…
ALL: [*screaming*] No!

*The phone rings. Lights up.*

UNCLE CHUK *enters and opens his mouth to speak.*

GRACE & MANOLO: [*together*] No! No! No! It's not your fault!

ROMAN *and* VATA *rush in and move in front of* UNCLE CHUK. *They stop and open their mouths to talk.*

No! 'We want a divorce blah, blah, blah…' No!

MANOLO *and* GRACE *giggle.*

*Blackout. The phone stops ringing.*

MANOLO: Don't worry—it's only a nightmare.
GRACE: I know. Can I open my eyes?
MANOLO: Wait till three: one… two… three.

*Lights up.*

ROMAN *and* VATA *are not there, but* UNCLE CHUK *stands where he was.* MANOLO *and* GRACE *look at him, surprised.*

Shit! Seems that we were only half asleep. His name should be NaGL.

GRACE *jumps under the table. She finds the guide book and starts crossing out the pages at a frantic pace.*

What book is that?
GRACE: Oh, c'mon. The Lonely Planet guide.
MANOLO: What's it about?
GRACE: Oh, c'mon! It's all about all the bloody things we can do in all the bloody places on Earth we can go…
MANOLO: 'We can go'? Can we go anywhere?
GRACE: Well: 'One can go'.
MANOLO: One? One can go? One!
GRACE: 'They can go'! Alright?

MANOLO: They? They can go to Vegas or they can go to hell! What I'm concerned with is: Can they come here? Is there anything about here in there? In the guide?

GRACE: There is a bit about everywhere…

MANOLO: Everywhere?! [*He grabs his head in a seizure of panic.*] So they know about everywhere.

GRACE: Correct. They might know about everywhere.

MANOLO: It means simply that there is nowhere to hide… There is no point to go anywhere, because they've been everywhere, they know everywhere, they will come everywhere… here.

*He notices that* GRACE *is still scratching and crossing out pages in the guide.*

What the hell are you doing?

GRACE: I'm getting rid of 'here'. So even if they find this Lonely Planet guide—there'll be no 'here' in it. Even if they want to come 'here'. Am I clear?

MANOLO: You're a fuckin' stupid genius of a bitch. Bloody hell! [*He remembers* UNCLE CHUK.] One of them is already here.

UNCLE CHUK *comes to life.*

UNCLE CHUK: I'm very sorry about the whole situation. It must be my fault. But from now on I'll try to be more from 'here' than you are, by celebrating the 'here day' in the following fashion: Firstly, I will recite the pledge of allegiance during a ceremony on the waterfront. I've done it so many times and in so many places that it shouldn't be a problem.

MANOLO: What do we do about him?

UNCLE CHUK: It's great to be from 'here'. With our friendliness, our 'have a go' attitude and our sense of humour we are famous throughout this Lonely Planet and what is a better time or place to celebrate being from 'here' than on the 'Here Day'.

UNCLE CHUK *starts playing didgeridoo.*

GRACE: He is only 'one'. I mentioned 'one' before, didn't I?

MANOLO: You said, 'One can go'.

GRACE: That's right. We can ignore 'one'. And we'll continue getting rid of 'here'.

UNCLE CHUK *quietly continues his mantra over the rest of the scene.*

UNCLE CHUK: For early birds there will be a traditional barbecue breakfast at the waterfront. For the patriotic ones there will be flag-raising ceremonies from coast to coast with politicians and officials and celebrities on display. Other highlights will include a First Fleet, bush ballads, dance callers, waterfront and children activities re-enactment, pie-eating competition, free rides for children under the age of fifteen, raft race, and the thong throwing contest followed by a billycart derby, highland dancing, magician/acrobat artist and hoola dancers. Restaurants and clubs across the country will also tuck into patriotic fervour with spit roasts, sausage sizzles, roo roasts and shrimps on a barbie on offer. Light up your barbecue, crack a tinny, Chuk (pardon my name) a few snags, share a joke and celebrate the best bloody nation on the Lonely Planet, where more languages are spoken in any capital city every bloody minute than in any other bloody city in the world. All you have to do to join in is to be eligible, and to be eligible, all you have to do is to be a permanent resident and have been 'here' as a permanent resident for two of the past five years, including twelve months in the past two years. You must be of good character, have a basic knowledge of the language spoken in 'Here', have an adequate knowledge of the responsibilities and privileges of being a 'Here' citizen and intent to live in, or maintain, a close and continuing association with 'Here'. Here—Here—Hooray! Here—Here—Hooray!

GRACE *and* MANOLO *continue to ignore the above monologue from* UNCLE CHUK *as they keep going with their conversation.*

MANOLO: We keep crossing out 'here', so they leave us in peace even if they'll find this bloody fuckin' 'Lonely Planet'.

GRACE: That's fuckin' wrong, mate. They won't leave us in peace, because they'd have to find us first, to leave us in peace, second. And they'll never find us in the first bloody place.

MANOLO: You're fuckin' brilliant. Give me the book.

*He helps her to cross out and rip out the pages in the book as the lights slowly go down.*

You never know, you… how brilliant you can be. So after there'll be no '*here*', they won't come here because there'll be no 'Here'. Wow! And then I'll fuck you dead, woman!

GRACE: And I won't even realise how lucky I'll be!

*By now* UNCLE CHUK*'s monologue comes to an end.*

*Blackout.*

*End Round Twenty-One.*

*ROUND TWENTY-TWO*

UNCLE CHUK *rings the bell.*

*The sound of a heavy punch landing on someone.*

*A sigh of relief.*

UNCLE CHUK, GRACE, MANOLO, VATA & ROMAN: [*together*] Here—Here—Hooray.

*Gong!*

*Lights down.*

*End of Round Twenty-Two.*

THE END

**Metanoia**

**presents**

***NaGL***

**7–17 October 2015**

Performers:

**Reece Vella**

**Miles Paras**

**Joseph Sherman**

**Judith Chaplin-Flemming**

Writer: **Lech Mackiewicz**

Director: **Greg Ulfan**

Designer: **Lara Week**

Lighting designer: **Shane Grant**

Dramaturg: **Gorkem Acaroglu**

**The Mechanics Institute is a Moreland City Council facility managed by Metanoia Theatre**

# LECH MACKIEWICZ

WRITER

Lech is a Polish actor, director and playwright. He is a graduate of the National Academy of Theatrical Arts (PWST) in Cracow and UTS, Sydney. He formed Auto Da Fe Theatre Co. in Sydney in 1987. His writing credits include: *NaGL*, *Everyman & The Pole Dancers*, *Ditto. A Story*, *Skierniewicer*, *Abba I Am Not*, *Felliniada*, *Shit Happens*. Lech has received three individual grants from the Australia Council for Arts. He is also the 1991 winner of a New South Wales Performing Arts Scholarship.

http://lechmackiewicz.com

**WRITER'S NOTE**

The play is called *NaGL* – an acronym for 'not a good look' – meaning: to describe something as unacceptable, foul, disastrous, inappropriate or awkward.

I believe that the dysfunctional family I portray in this theatrical metaphor fits the acronym, and, by implication, so does Australian society.

*NaGL* is my personal experience. Although *NaGL* is not a factual record of events, *NaGL* is a true story of what happened to my family, to the way we are, to the way we see the world and its progress (or regress). *NaGL* sounds absurd on the first read, but after a while the absurdity of it takes a very real shape – the shape of our everydayness.

*NaGL* rules. *NaGL* surrounds us. *NaGL* is what is happening to us.

It is funny, but is it really?

## GREG ULFAN

DIRECTOR

A graduate of the Victorian College of the Arts (VCA), Greg has worked as an actor and a director with a range of Australian theatre companies including Not Yet It's Difficult (NYID), Melbourne Theatre Company (MTC), Malthouse, Sydney Theatre Company (STC), La Mama, and has appeared in an array of Australian TV shows. He has also worked for over ten years as an interpreter and actor with Russian theatre director, Professor Leonid Verzub (a student and co-worker of Maria Knebl). When he's not working on shows, Greg can be seen teaching and running actors' workshops.

## REECE VELLA

ACTOR

Reece graduated from The Actors College of Theatre and TV in Sydney in 2010 and has been acting professionally for the past five years, working with the likes of Lech Mackiewicz, Lex Marinos and Mario Philip Azzopardi. With a passion for new work, some of his latest endeavors include: the world premiere of *Il- Kappillan ta' Malta* in Malta, *Everyman and the Pole Dancers* at Metanoia Theatre, the sellout *Tales of a City by the Sea* at La Mama Courthouse and *Between Heaven and Her* at La Mama. Reece is delighted to be performing again at Metanoia, holding true to its creed of creating a change of perception.

## MILES PARAS

ACTOR

Having graduated from WAAPA, Miles has worked in television, film and on stage. TV credits include *Wentworth 3*, *City Homicide 2&3* and *Carla Cametti*. Miles recently worked with Chi Vu in Metanoia Theatre's production of 10Cs. She has also worked for MTC, Short & Sweet and Bell Shakespeare. This year has been a pleasure having more time to pursue performance after spending the recent years raising a young family.

## JOSEPH SHERMAN

ACTOR

Joseph Sherman is a graduate from the John Bolton Theatre School and combines acting and theatre making with medical practice as a General Practitioner. Over the last five years he has produced, co-devised and performed in extensive collaborations (*Lower Depths*, *The Tempest*, *Our Chalk Circle* and *Dante's Workshop*) with St Kilda Uniting Care. Greg has directed him as Uncle Vanya and in two incarnations of *Roulette*. Joseph and Greg are founding member of Inotrope Productions, formed in 2002 with Russian Soup (directed by John Bolton).

# JUDITH CHAPLIN-FLEMMING

ACTOR

Judith studied at the University of Tasmania and began her working life as an actor. A graduate of NIDA, Judith has worked in film, TV and stage, both as an actor, director, producer and writer. She has worked in the UK, America and South East Asia. Recently Judith performed, wrote and produced her own play which was presented in a sold out season as part of the Melbourne Fringe Festival.

# LARA WEEK

DESIGNER

Lara is a producer and designer for performance. In 2013, Lara completed her PG Dip in Performance Creation (Design) at the Victorian College of the Arts. Her design credits include: *Between Heaven and Her* (La Mama Theatre), *Tales of a City by the Sea* (La Mama Courthouse), *The Conference of the Birds* (Centre for Cultural Partnerships), *A Feat Incomplete* (Old 505 Theatre) and *Tzlilei Kesem* (Israeli Opera). Since 2011, she has been associate producer for Tribal Soul Arts, producing decolonial arts programs and performances in Zimbabwe, Mozambique, the Netherlands, UK, and Australia. She is dedicated to creating spaces where people with different skills and perspectives can share ideas and produce work together.

## SHANE GRANT

LIGHTING DESIGNER

Shane is an accomplished lighting designer having worked extensively with companies like Ranters Theatre, The Torch Project, NYID and many others. With a BA Dramatic Arts (Production) Victorian College of the Arts (VCA), Shane was previously Production Manager with Strange Fruit, and Technical Manager at Gasworks Theatre. He is currently the Audio Visual Technician for St Kevin's College, a position that he has held for eight years.

## GORKEM ACAROGLU

DRAMATURG

Gorkem Acaroglu is a theatre maker, most passionate about work that tests the borders of traditional form and content. She is Creative Director of The 24 Hour Experience – a living documentary through the hidden perspectives of place, which premiered in Melbourne. Gorkem has had an ongoing interest in the capacity of digital technologies to perform alongside live actors and explored this through an Australia Council Artlab initiative working with robotics and motion capture technologies. In 2012 Gorkem travelled to Mongolia through Asialink and worked with local theatre makers to develop a documentary -style Mongolian perspective of Hamlet. Gorkem was an inaugural Sidney Myer Creative Fellow and is currently completing her PhD at Deakin University examining the capacity for technological actors to perform competently with human actors on stage.